CATERPILLAR

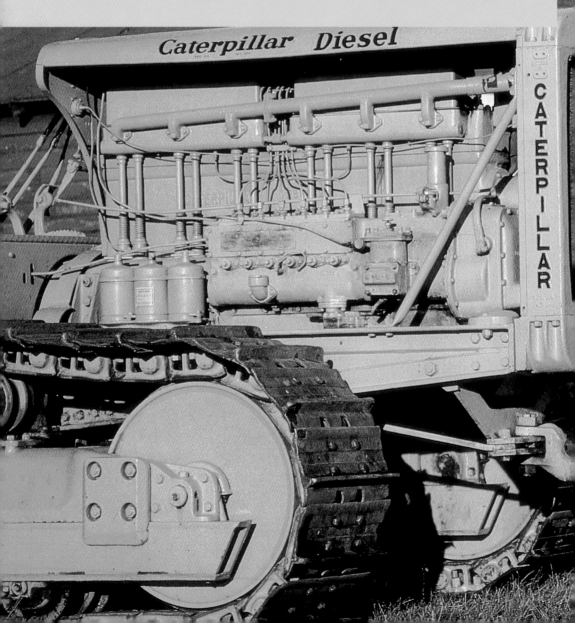

First published in 2006 by Motorbooks, an imprint of MBI Publishing Company, Galtier Plaza, Suite 200, 380 Jackson Street, St. Paul, MN 55101-3885 USA

The information in this book is true and complete to the best of our knowledge. All recommendations are made without any guarantee on the part of the author or Publisher, who also disclaim any liability incurred in connection with the use of this data or specific details.

This publication has not been prepared, approved, or licensed by Caterpillar Inc.

We recognize, further, that some words, model names, and designations mentioned herein are the property of the trademark holder. We use them for identification purposes only. This is not an official publication.

MBI Publishing Company titles are also available at discounts in bulk quantity for industrial or sales-promotional use. For details write to Special Sales Manager at MBI Publishing Company, Galtier Plaza, Suite 200, 380 Jackson Street, St. Paul, MN 55101-3885 USA

ISBN-13: 978-0-7603-2553-7
ISBN-10: 0-7603-2553-7

Editor: Steve Gansen
Designer: LeAnn Kuhlmann
Printed in China

About the Author

Eric C. Orlemann has authored such works as *Giant Earth-Moving Equipment*, *Euclid and Terex*, *Super-Duty Earthmovers*, *Caterpillar Chronicle*, *LeTourneau Earthmovers*, *Building Giant Earthmovers*, *Colossal Caterpillar*, and *The Caterpillar Century* for MBI Publishing Company. He has also contributed numerous articles to *Equipment Echoes*, the Historical Construction Equipment Association's official newsmagazine. Orlemann has served as technical consultant for heavy equipment-related programs appearing on the History Channel, the Learning Channel (TLC), and the Discovery Channel. He lives in Decatur, Illinois.

On the front cover: Since its unveiling in late 1998, the Caterpillar 797 series of off-highway haulers has become the world's best-selling ultra-hauler in the 360-plus-ton category.

On the frontispiece: The 797 is the largest mechanical-drive hauler in the world and is capable of hauling payloads approaching 400 tons in weight.

On the title page: Two of Caterpillar's historical icons, the Seventy-Five and its replacement, the RD8, are some of the company's most beloved diesel track-type tractors.

On the acknowledgments page: Peoria, Illinois, the location of Caterpillar's world headquarters, is often referred to as "the earth-moving capital of the world." Just southeast of Peoria is Decatur, home to Cat's assembly plant for all of its rigid haul truck, motor grader, and scraper model lines.

Contents

ACKNOWLEDGMENTS

I would like to thank the many individuals, currently working and retired, of Caterpillar Inc., who over the years have taken a keen interest in helping me with my many endeavors showcasing the company's various achievements. Without their help and support, many of these projects would never have gotten off the ground.

I would also like to thank the many tractor owners whose vintage machines appear in these pages. Their work is truly a labor of love and devotion to Caterpillar and its predecessors, Holt and Best.

Special thanks are also in order to Joe Keen, Dave Peters, and Kirk Wesley of Altorfer Cat for providing various pieces of equipment for photographic purposes. I would also like to express my sincerest appreciation to Jim Patterson of the American Asphalt & Grading Company for granting me access to their many jobsites in pursuit of the "yellow iron."

Lastly, I would like to thank my good friends Gary Middlebrook, Tim Twichell, Nick Cedar, Urs Peyer, and Thomas Wilk for providing additional photographic images of Caterpillar equipment in use in Canada and various European countries. I couldn't have done it without you guys.

—Eric C. Orlemann
Decatur, Illinois, 2006

Introduced at the 2004 MINExpo, the 994F is the largest front-end wheel loader ever manufactured by the company as of 2006.

Introduction—Holt and Best

Recently, Caterpillar celebrated the 100th anniversary of its involvement with the track-type tractor design. It was on November 24, 1904, that the very first Holt prototype steam-powered crawler tractor was tested under its own power at the company's plant in Stockton, California. The Holt Manufacturing Company was one of the founding companies that would become the Caterpillar Tractor Company. The other firm in this equation was Best Manufacturing of San Leandro, California. The early tractor and harvester designs of these two pioneering companies would lay the groundwork for a firm that would eventually become the largest manufacturer of heavy equipment the world has ever known.

The Holt Manufacturing Company's origins date back to 1883, when a gentleman by the name of Benjamin Holt, along with his brothers, founded the Stockton Wheel Company. The company's main products were wagon wheels and other small agricultural tools. But soon the company's attention would focus on the development of a combine featuring linked chains and sprockets instead of belt-driven pulley systems. Holt started experimental design work on this new combine design in 1885. By 1886, the company

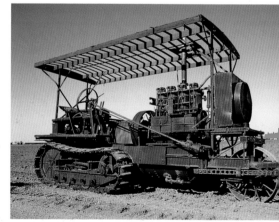

Originally manufactured in 1908, this 25-horsepower Holt 40, carrying serial number 1004, was the second gas-powered crawler tractor sold by the company. It is the oldest known surviving Holt crawler model in the world today.

was able to introduce its first model, "The Holt Bros. Improved Link Belt Combined Harvester." The new Holt combines' use of a link-belt design made the unit far more reliable and quieter, which lessened the likelihood of startling the horse teams. In the past, runaway horse teams had posed a major threat to the well-being of the operators and their harvesters alike.

Holt realized that the horse teams were the weak link in the future of mechanized harvesting. Holt's answer to this dilemma was an industry first—the 1890 introduction of the company's first steam traction engine featuring steering clutches. Nicknamed "Old Betsy," the traction engine would usher in an entire new product line for the company and prove once and for all that mechanization, not animal power, was the future for the agricultural industry. In 1892, the Holt brothers changed the name of their firm to the Holt

Manufacturing Company and appointed Benjamin as president of the operation.

But even as Holt was introducing new combine and tractor designs, another entrepreneur by the name of Daniel Best was also charting a parallel course in the manufacture of tractor-pulled harvesters. In 1869, Best started a job working at his older brother's ranch in Marysville, California. While at the ranch, Daniel invented a transportable cleaner machine for that year's grain harvest. So successful was the design that Best applied for a patent on his invention, which was awarded to him in April 1871. But Best was a restless man who was always looking for better ways of making a fortune, including a stint at gold mining and making design improvements to clothes washing machines. But around 1880, Best was back at the drawing board designing larger, more productive harvesters for the farmers of California. Best's

The Holt 75 was manufactured both in Stockton, California, and in Peoria, Illinois. This Stockton-built Holt 75 Model T8 was in production from 1916 to 1921. It was primarily designed for agricultural use. Most of the Peoria-built tractors (1914 to 1918) were for wartime needs.

This restored Stockton-built 1917 vintage Holt 45 Model T10 was commonly referred to as a "muley," which was farm slang for a cow without horns. This was in reference to the removal of the front tiller wheel in this Holt tractor design.

new designs combined the process of harvesting, cleaning, and bagging in one unit. Combines of this nature existed out east, but not on the scale of the Best machine. In 1886, Best established a larger manufacturing operation in San Leandro, California, called "Daniel Best Agricultural Works." In 1888, Best purchased the rights to build the Remington "Rough and Ready" steam traction engine. By February 1889, Best introduced his own tractor design large enough to pull his company's large harvesters. The dawn of high-production mechanized farming was now at hand.

For the next 18 years, both companies would introduce numerous designs of steam traction engines and combine harvesters. Almost model for model, both companies countered each others' offerings. But the one area Holt was ahead of Best centered on the development of a track-type tractor. The wheeled steamers of the day, fitted with extra-wide high-floatation wheels, were

In 1919, C. L. Best introduced his legendary Best 60, which would eventually evolve into one of the most famous gasoline-powered crawler tractors of all time, the Caterpillar Sixty.

simply becoming too large in the field. A belted crawler track seemed the logical answer to the problem. Even though Holt did not necessarily invent the first crawler track design (that honor goes to Lombard), the company was responsible for refining the concept into a production machine. Holt tested his first crawler track steamer in November 1904. After more testing and further design modifications, Holt finally sold its first crawler model, the "Holt Brothers Paddle Wheel Improved Traction Engine," in late 1906. Other key technological advances made by Holt included the introduction of gasoline-powered tractors. Holt built its first prototype gas-powered tractor in December 1906. But it would not be until the fall of 1908 that the first one (Model 40 S.N. 1003) was sold and shipped to a paying customer.

As competition heated up between the two companies, a patent infringement lawsuit filed by Best against Holt in 1905 pitted the firms against each other in court. After a few years of hearings, both companies decided to settle their differences out of court. This out-of-court settlement also initiated talks between the firms about the feasibility of merging the two companies into one. Daniel Best thought it was in his best interest at this time in his life to sell Best Manufacturing to Holt. On October 8, 1908, Best sold his company to Holt with the agreement that his son, Clarence Leo Best, would become president of Holt Manufacturing Company's San Leandro facilities.

After two years of working for Holt, C. L. Best decided that a change was in order. Dissatisfied with the working relationship he had with Holt's board of directors, C. L. Best left the company in 1910 to start his own tractor line, which would put the Best name once again in competition with Holt. Initially, the C. L. Best Gas Traction Company offered wheel-type gasoline-powered tiller-wheel tractors. In late 1912, the company introduced its first tiller-wheel track-type tractor model—the C.L.B. 70-horsepower "Tracklayer." This model would lead to a more powerful and refined C.L.B. 75 Tracklayer in 1914.

Even though C. L. Best Tracklayers were in direct competition with Holt's "Caterpillar" models (the term "Caterpillar" was officially registered as a company trademark in 1910), Holt offered a far broader range of tiller-wheeled crawler tractors to choose from. Popular model lines included the Holt 18 Midget (1914), the Baby 30 (1912), the 60 (1911), the 75 (1913), and the 120 (1914). In late 1913, Holt offered the company's first "muley" tractor design—the 20-30 Model T5 (also referred to as a Holt Baby). This was quickly followed up in 1914 by a more refined Holt 45 Model T10 tillerless-wheel design. The 45 proved to be popular not only in a farmer's field, but in the battlefields of Europe as well. Other popular Holt "muley" tractor designs of the time included the Model 55 (1917), the 2-Ton Model T35 (1921), the 5-Ton Model T11 (1917), and the 10-Ton Model T16 (1918).

Even though C. L. Best may not have beaten Holt to the marketplace with the first tillerless-wheel track-type tractor design, he did introduce "muley" tractor models of his own. Popular models of these included the C. L. Best 25 H.P. (1918) and the 40 H.P. Tracklayers (1914). But the real groundbreaking models were his 30 (1921) and 60 (1919) Tracklayer tractors. Modern in design, reliable in operation, they would be the agricultural tractors of choice for years to come.

After the signing of the armistice that ended World War I in November 1918, a wave of military surplus tractors flooded the marketplace; additionally, many of Holt's military contracts were cancelled. Since Holt was one of the major suppliers of tractors during the war, the situation placed enormous financial burdens on the company. During this time, C. L. Best was not fairing much better in the marketplace. The availability of cheap surplus tractors weakened the company considerably. In the early 1920s, both companies faced the real possibility of failure. If they were to survive in the changing marketplace, drastic measures would have to be taken. So on April 15, 1925, the Holt Manufacturing Co. and

Though not as large as its bigger brother, the Best 30 would become another crawler tractor historical milestone with its introduction in 1921.

the C. L. Best Tractor Co. officially merged together to form a new combined and stronger manufacturing entity—the Caterpillar Tractor Company.

It has been over 80 years since this historic day in Caterpillar history. As the decades have passed, Caterpillar has evolved from simply being known as a tractor manufacturer to being a global leader in the development and production of heavy equipment, engines, and various other technical and financial support services. Along with the company's classic earthmoving product lines, Caterpillar's other varied offerings include telehandlers; track and wheel material handlers; underground mining equipment; forestry machines such as skidders, feller bunchers, and track harvesters; vibratory soil, asphalt, and pneumatic compactors; and asphalt paving equipment, to name but a few. Caterpillar state-of-the-art diesel engines can not only be found in their products, but also in countless thousands of various makes of over-the-road trucks and equipment. The company also invests heavily in future technology and development research programs, keeping Caterpillar at the forefront of heavy equipment design for the challenges awaiting it in the twenty-first century.

Track-Type
Tractors

Track-Type Tractors

On April 15, 1925, the Caterpillar Tractor Company was born. Key to the company's future success would be its track-type tractors built in San Leandro, California, and in Peoria, Illinois. At this time in the company's history, the only products marketed by Caterpillar were tractors (Harvesters were sold under the Holt Harvester Works name, which became a wholly owned subsidiary company in 1926, known as the Western Harvester Company). Caterpillar's initial track-type tractor offerings were a selection of older Best and Holt models. The Best 30 and 60 became the Caterpillar Thirty and Sixty, respectively. For the older Holt tractors, only the 2-Ton, 5-Ton, and 10-Ton tractor models remained. The Sixty and 10-Ton were very close performance wise in the new lineup. The 10-Ton was also a more complicated tractor to manufacture at the time, so it was only natural that this model would be the first to be phased out of production by 1926. The next to get the axe was the 5-Ton, which ended its run at the end of 1926. Of greater importance to the company

was the new Twenty model from 1927. The Twenty was Caterpillar's first tractor design that was not based on a previous Best or Holt model. It was a pure Caterpillar tractor through and through.

The year 1931 proved to be a pivotal one in the history of Caterpillar and track-type tractors as a whole. In September, Caterpillar shipped its first diesel engine–powered tractor, the Diesel Sixty. The advantage of a diesel engine over a gasoline-powered unit was the diesel's superior low-end torque. Even though the acceptance of the diesel engine–powered track-type tractor was slow in the industry at first, it soon proved itself as the powertrain of choice by the late 1930s. Caterpillar ended production of its last commercial gasoline-powered tractor, the R4, in 1944.

During the 1950s, the company's tractors were known more as heavy-construction, earthmoving machines and less as agricultural tools. This was made perfectly clear in 1955 with the release of the legendary model D9D. The D9D was the first all-new model class of tractor introduced by the company since the 1930s. Over the years, the company's tractor upgrades were based on a previous model, but the D9D was all new from the ground up. Its principal customers were large quarry and mining operations.

In the 1970s, Caterpillar would practically rewrite the book on track-type tractor design with the introduction of the mighty D10. Officially introduced in the fall of 1977, the D10 featured Caterpillar's first use of its elevated drive sprocket system. Even though the concept of this track drive design had been around for decades, it had never been utilized in a tractor the size of the D10. Soon all of the company's major crawlers would feature the elevated drive sprocket system.

With the introduction of the N-series crawler tractors in 1987, Caterpillar made a slight realignment of its model lines. The D10 became the D11N, the D9L became the D10N, and the D8L was transformed into the D9N. To fill the void in the product line left vacant by the D8L, an entirely new D8N model was introduced.

The latest Caterpillar track-type tractor offerings are the new T-series designs. The new T-series are some of the most technologically advanced and productive crawlers in the company's history. And they are environmentally friendly, too, thanks to their use of low-emission Cat ACERT diesel engine technology. The company's first T-series tractors were released in 2004.

The company's track-type tractor designs over the years have also included pipe-layer and logging configurations, as well as track loaders in various sizes and bucket capacities. Caterpillar even offered a rubber-tracked model in 1986. Referred to as the Challenger, it featured the company's Mobil-trac System (MTS) and was primarily marketed as an agricultural tractor. Caterpillar would eventually sell the design, assembly, and marketing rights to its Challenger product line in December 2001 to AGCO of Georgia. In December 2002, Caterpillar also sold the rights of its rubber-belted track component business to Camoplast of Quebec, Canada. Today's current MT-series of Challenger MTS tractors are sold in North America under the Cat name under a license agreement and feature engines and drivetrains designed and supplied by Caterpillar, Inc.

The popular Caterpillar 2-Ton Model T35 tractor series can trace its roots back to the Holt 2-Ton originally introduced in 1921. In April 1925, it became a Caterpillar model. Production would last until 1928. *Nick Cedar*

In March 1905, company photographer Charles Clements saw Holt's prototype track-type road engine at work for the first time. He exclaimed aloud to Benjamin Holt, "If that don't look like a monster caterpillar," the first use of "caterpillar" to describe the tractor.

The Caterpillar 5-Ton Model T29 was another of the early Holt designs that would carry over into the new Caterpillar era. The 5-Ton series was originally introduced by Holt in 1917 with the Model T11 military tractor. Production on the Caterpillar 5-Ton ended in 1926.

The 10-Ton Model T16 was the largest of the early Holt tractor designs to become a Caterpillar model in 1925. The Holt 10-Ton shown was almost the same as its Caterpillar counterpart except for the casting designs on the sides of the radiator. Production would end by 1926. *Nick Cedar*

TRACTORS

Originally introduced in 1921 as the Best 30, the Caterpillar Thirty was born in 1925 after the merger of the Best and Holt companies. It would remain in production until 1932.

The Caterpillar Thirty and Sixty crawler tractors originally started life out as C. L. Best models, the Best 30 and Best 60.

The most famous of the early Caterpillar gasoline-powered tractor models was the Sixty. Derived from the Best 60 of 1919, it would remain in production until 1931.

The Caterpillar Sixty was powered by a big 50-horsepower, four-cylinder 6 1/2x8 1/2-inch bore and stroke, valve-in-head gasoline engine, which was considered very reliable in operation for its day.

The first tractor model to be entirely designed by Caterpillar engineers and not based on a previous Holt or Best unit was the Twenty from 1927. This early Twenty was built in San Leandro (S.N. prefix L) from 1927 to 1929, and in Peoria (S.N. prefix PL) from 1928 to 1932.

In late 1928, Caterpillar replaced its aging smaller 2-Ton tractor with the newly designed Ten. The Ten was actually a bit smaller than the outgoing 2-Ton, but proved very popular with orchard farmers because of its ability to work between the trees.

The model Twenty from 1927 was the Caterpillar Tractor Company's first track-type tractor not based on a previous Holt or Best design.

Caterpillar built two entirely different tractor model lines that carried the "Fifteen" nomenclature. Pictured on the left is a model Fifteen (S.N. prefix PV) that was manufactured from 1928 to 1932. On the right is the "small" Fifteen (S.N. prefix 7C), which was in production from 1932 to 1933.

The Caterpillar Ten "high-clearance" configuration was offered at the same time as the regular Ten. Only 395 Ten tractors were built this way.

Caterpillar's high-clearance tractors were built for farmers who needed the extra clearance height of the tractor chassis for cultivating and other row crop field work.

Caterpillar replaced the Ten "high-clearance" with the model Fifteen (S.N. prefix 1D). The Fifteen "high-clearance" was based on the "small" Fifteen (7C) tractor model. Only 95 were built between 1932 and 1933.

Rarest of all the smaller row crop tractors built by Caterpillar was the Twenty-Two "high-clearance." Only a handful of these were known to have been built. The Twenty-Two series was in production from 1934 to 1939.

Introduced in 1932, the gasoline-powered Caterpillar Sixty-Five (2D) is unique in the company's history as being the only tractor model to be designed with this "rounded" look. Production ended in 1933.

Largest of all the gasoline-powered tractor designs built by Caterpillar was the Seventy (8D). Manufactured from 1933 to 1937, the Seventy was the replacement for the gas Sixty-Five model. *Nick Cedar*

The big Seventy was powered by a Cat 9500G, four-cylinder gasoline engine, rated at 77.07 drawbar horsepower. In all, only 266 examples were ever produced. *Nick Cedar*

Early Large Gas Tractors				
Model	Build Year	Engine	Horsepower Belt/Drawbar	Weight (pounds)
Sixty	1919 (Best)	6 1/2x8 1/2 inch	60/50	19,000
Sixty-Five	1932	9000G	79/68	23,007
Seventy	1933	9500G	89.43/77.07	29,540

The Caterpillar R3 is another one of the company's very rare track-type tractors. Manufactured between 1934 and 1935, only 60 examples of this gasoline-powered model were ever produced.

Introduced in 1934, the Caterpillar R2 was produced in three different serial number lots, with production ending in 1942. Most of the R-series tractors were for governmental and forestry service use, but many also found their way into the private sector as well. *Caterpillar Inc. Corporate Archives*

The majority of R-series gasoline powered tractor models built by Caterpillar were originally produced for various U.S. government agencies, such as the forestry service, during the 1930s and early 1940s. Models included the R2, R3, R4, R5, and R6.

The Caterpillar R4 series was actually the continuation of the gas-powered Thirty (6G) tractor line from late 1935. Only the nomenclature was different. Production on the R4 lasted from 1938 to 1944.

One of Caterpillar's most significant track-type tractor models was its revolutionary Diesel Sixty. Pictured is the second tractor built (1C2) in fully restored condition. Only the first two Diesel Sixty units were painted this way, and both were the only ones built at the San Leandro plant in 1931. *Nick Cedar*

Caterpillar officially changed its standard equipment colors from gray to Cat Hi-Way Yellow on December 7, 1931. A Cat Silver-Gray, trimmed in black color scheme was also available as a no-cost option.

Of Caterpillar's early Diesel tractors, "Old Tusko" is without a doubt, the most famous of them all. In March and April 1932, this Diesel Sixty (S.N. 1C12) set world records for nonstop plowing achievements in Arlington, Oregon.

Powering "Old Tusko" was a Cat D9900, four-cylinder diesel engine, rated at 70.25 drawbar horsepower and 83.86 belt horsepower. This was Caterpillar's first production diesel engine design.

During the production run of the Diesel Sixty, the casting "SIXTY" on the sides of the radiator started to be replaced with "DIESEL." By the end of the production run, the tractor was referred to as the Diesel Sixty-Five.

The Diesel Sixty/Sixty-Five was just at home on a construction site as it was in the field. Most would agree that the Diesel Sixty was the single most important track-type tractor design ever produced by Caterpillar. *Caterpillar Inc. Corporate Archives*

The Diesel Sixty was Caterpillar's first production diesel-powered track-type tractor model.

The Diesel Sixty/Sixty-Five was in production from 1931 to 1932, with a grand total of only 157 units being built. They are some of the most collectable diesel tractors in the world today.

In 1933, Caterpillar introduced the Diesel Seventy (3E) as a replacement for the Diesel Sixty-Five. It was equipped with a slightly more powerful D9900 diesel engine than the one found in the previous model. Production ended in late 1933 with only 51 tractors built. *Author's collection*

The Diesel Seventy's replacement was the far superior Diesel Seventy-Five (2E). Gone was the diesel D9900 engine. In its place was the newly designed D11000, six-cylinder diesel, rated at 83.23 drawbar horsepower and 98.01 belt horsepower. *Author's collection*

Early Large Diesel Tractors				
Model	Build Year	Engine	Horsepower Belt/Drawbar	Weight (pounds)
Diesel Sixty	1931	D9900	79/68	24,390
Diesel Seventy	1933	D9900	87/76	30,800
Diesel Seventy-Five	1933	D11000	98.01/83.23	32,600

The Diesel Seventy-Five was in production from 1933 to 1935, with a total of 1,078 tractors listed as being produced. It would be replaced by the RD8 in 1935.

The smallest diesel-powered track-type tractor to be built by Caterpillar was its very popular D2 model line. The D2 (3J and 5J) was originally introduced in 1938. Pictured is a fully restored vintage 1939 (3J) model.

In 1947, Caterpillar introduced a new D2 model equipped with a Cat D311, four-cylinder diesel engine. It was available in 40-inch (4U) and 50-inch (5U) track gauges. The two series of D2 tractors were built from 1938 to 1947 (3J/5J) and 1947 to 1957 (4U/5U). The unit pictured is a vintage 1955 (5U) D2 equipped with a rear-seat-mounted fuel tank.

The Caterpillar D2 model series was the smallest diesel-powered track-type tractor ever offered by the company to go into full production.

The diesel-powered Caterpillar RD4 (4G) was originally released in 1936. In 1937, its designation would be changed to simply D4. The RD4 shown is equipped with an R.G. LeTourneau C4 Angledozer.

In 1986, Caterpillar changed its corporate name from the "Caterpillar Tractor Company" to simply "Caterpillar Inc." Then, in 1989, it introduced two new corporate trademark designs that featured a yellow triangle symbol incorporated into the letter "A" of the words "CAT" and "CATERPILLAR."

The early D4 model lines were some of the most popular track-type tractors ever sold by Caterpillar. The RD4/D4 was in production from 1936 to 1959 with an astounding 94,496 tractors of all types listed as being produced.

The D5 model line actually started in 1939, but ended production in that same year. The D5 would once again be added to the product line in 1966, and it has been there in its many forms ever since. Pictured is a current D5N XL. *Urs Peyer*

The first D5 (S.N. prefix 9M) track-type tractor was built by Caterpillar in 1939, and was based on a D6 model fitted with a special D4 chassis with five track rollers. Only 46 were ever produced, all in 1939.

The D5H LGP Series II was an ideal tractor for working in wet or muddy conditions due to its Low Ground Pressure (LGP) undercarriage. It would be replaced by the D5M series in 1996. *Urs Peyer*

Officially introduced in 2001, the Caterpillar D5G LGP is a slightly smaller tractor than the current D5N series. The D5G series utilizes a hydrostatic drive system and a conventional track undercarriage design. *Urs Peyer*

The D6N LGP is a very specialized tractor, perfect for working in unstable areas where higher flotation is required. The first full year of production for the D6N series was 2003. *Urs Peyer*

During World War II, Caterpillar produced two military variation D6 tractors. One was the High Speed D6, Tractor M1, and the other was a factory-armored D6A.

Caterpillar's D6 series of track-type tractors dates back to the RD6 from 1935. In 1937, the nomenclature would change to simply D6. The original D6 series was in production until 1959. Pictured is a vintage 1955 D6 (8U). *Thomas Wilk*

Because of its compact size, the D6 was well suited for agricultural field work. This late 1950s D6 is equipped with a Cat No. 64 Tool Bar with three plowing shanks. *Author's collection*

In 1935, Caterpillar introduced the RD7, which would ultimately become the D7 in 1937. The most popular of these early tractors was the 3T series produced between 1944 and 1955. Pictured is a 1954 vintage D7 (3T). *Thomas Wilk*

| Select D7 Models | | | | |
Model	Build Year	Engine	Horsepower Gross/Flywheel	Weight (pounds)
D7D	1959	D339	—/140	33,015
D7E	1961	D339	—/180	40,085
D7F	1969	3306	—/180	40,300
D7G	1975	3306	—/200	44,300
D7H	1985	3306	231/215	50,246
D7H II	1990	3306	247/230	54,511
D7R	1995	3306	247/230	54,200
D7R II	2001	3176C	258/240	54,582

The first RD7 (5E7501) was introduced in 1935, which was followed up with an improved version (9G) in that same year. Its production would last until 1937. Pictured is a fully restored 1936 vintage RD7.

Numerous models of D7 tractor lines have been produced over the decades by Caterpillar. The D7F shown was originally introduced in 1969 and was in production through 1974. It was replaced by the D7G in 1975. *Author's collection*

Introduced in late 1958, Caterpillar's D8H was a formidable track-type tractor. It was offered in direct drive, torque converter, or power shift transmission configurations. Pictured is a 1965 (46A) vintage D8H equipped with power shift. *Urs Peyer*

The RD8/D8 was the largest track-type tractor series offered by Caterpillar until the introduction of the D9D in 1955.

Caterpillar's largest tractor offering in the 1930s and 1940s was the RD8/D8 model series. The original RD8 was introduced in 1935 and was changed to simply D8 in 1937. The RD8 replaced the Diesel Seventy-Five.

Caterpillar made significant changes to the D8 in 1955 with the introduction of the Series D with torque converter drive and Series E with direct drive. *Urs Peyer*

Introduced in 2004, the D8T is the most productive D8 series tractor ever produced. At its heart is a new low-emission Cat C15 ACERT diesel engine, rated at 310 flywheel horsepower. *Urs Peyer*

Select D8 Models

Model	Build Year	Engine	Horsepower Gross/Flywheel	Weight (pounds)
D8H	1958	D342	—/270	62,000
D8K	1974	D342	—/300	70,500
D8L	1981	3408	—/335	84,010
D8N	1987	3406C	306/285	82,590
D8R	1995	3406E	328/305	82,850
D8R II	2001	3406E	338/310	83,500
D8T	2004	C15 ACERT	347/310	84,850

In 1974, Caterpillar replaced its very popular D8H with the equally impressive model D8K. The D8K was the last of the conventionally designed undercarriages before the introduction of the elevated drive D8L. Production ended on the D8K in 1982. *Author's collection*

Caterpillar's popular elevated drive model D8R was originally introduced in 1995 as a replacement for the D8N. Pictured is a 310 flywheel horsepower D8R Series II introduced in 2000. *Urs Peyer*

Caterpillar's legendary D9 series of large crawler tractors was originally introduced to the public in 1955. The D9D series would remain in production until 1959. *Author's collection*

The D9G was originally introduced in 1961 as a replacement for the D9E series. The D9G featured a power shift transmission and was rated at 385 flywheel horsepower. *Author's collection*

The D9E from 1959 was the first of the D9 series to offer a full-power shift transmission option, which allowed the operator to shift on-the-go, and under full load, with a single lever.

In 1974, the D9G was replaced with an improved and more powerful model D9H. The D9H was rated at 410 flywheel horsepower and featured an optional modular ROPS cab. Production would end on the D9H in 1981.

The D9L was introduced in 1980 and was the first D9 series tractor to feature the new elevated sprocket drive system. *Caterpillar Inc. Corporate Archives*

Introduced in 1987, the model D9N was not necessarily a replacement for the D9L, but was in fact the replacement for the D8L instead. The D9N was rated at 370 flywheel horsepower. *Urs Peyer*

The Caterpillar D9T is the latest entry into the legendary D9 series hall of fame. Released in 2004, the D9T is powered by a newly designed Cat C18 ACERT diesel engine, rated at 410 flywheel horsepower. *Caterpillar Inc.*

Starting with the D9L in 1980, all D9 series track-type tractors featured Caterpillar's elevated drive-sprocket system.

The first Quad-Trac D9G was designed by Buster Peterson of the Peterson Tractor Company in San Leandro, California, in late 1963. It is pictured here at work in March 1964. *Peterson Tractor*

The DD9G/H push-pull dozer was controlled by a single operator from the front tractor. When needed, both tractors could be separated and operated independently from each other.

The original design concept of the Quad-Trac D9Gs was purchased by Caterpillar from Buster Peterson and in 1968 was marketed as the DD9G. In 1974, the DD9G was replaced by the more powerful DD9H series. *Thomas Wilk*

The original DD9G was rated at 770 flywheel horsepower. Its replacement, the DD9H, was rated at 820. Production ended on the DD9H in 1980. *Thomas Wilk*

The invention of the Quad-Trac D9G eventually led to a side-by-side version being built as well. Caterpillar introduced a production SxS D9G in late 1969. It was rated at 770 flywheel horsepower. *Caterpillar, Inc.*

D9G and H Model Lines				
Model	Build Year	Engine	Horsepower Flywheel	Weight (pounds)
D9G	1961	D353	385	99,500*
D9H	1974	D353	410	107,230*
DD9G	1963 (Pederson)			
	1968 (Cat)	D353 (x2)	770	176,900
DD9H	1974	D353 (x2)	820	178,800
SxS D9G	1969	D353 (x2)	770	188,600
SxS D9H	1974	D353 (x2)	820	183,900

*includes blade, ROPS, and ripper

In mid-1974, the SxS D9H replaced the previous G series model. With its 24-foot-wide bulldozing blade, it was the perfect dozer for large mining land reclamation jobs.

Only one operator in the left tractor controlled all functions of the SxS D9H. The original SxS D9G was rated at 770 flywheel horsepower and the H model at 820. Production ended in 1977.

The Caterpillar D10 was the company's first track-type tractor model to feature the newly designed elevated drive-sprocket system.

The original Caterpillar D10 was a monster in its day. No other dozer looked like it or performed like it. Rated at 700 flywheel horsepower, the D10 could pull its massive 6-foot ripper shank through solid rock like a hot knife through butter. *Caterpillar Inc.*

The D10 was officially announced by Caterpillar in 1977, with full production getting underway in the spring of 1978. *Caterpillar Inc.*

Caterpillar's D10R model series was officially introduced in 1996 as the replacement for the D10N. The D10R was powered by a Cat 3412E, 12-cylinder diesel engine rated at 570 flywheel horsepower.

The D10N, introduced in 1987, was not a replacement for the D10, but was in fact the replacement for the D9L instead.

Introduced in 1987, the D10N was rated at 520 flywheel horsepower.

In 2004, the model D10R was replaced by the D10T. The D10T is powered by a newly designed EPA Tier 3 emissions compliant Cat C27 ACERT diesel engine, rated at 580 flywheel horsepower. *Urs Peyer*

The current D11R and D11R CD "Carrydozer" models are the most powerful track-type tractors ever offered by Caterpillar. Each dozer is rated at 850 flywheel horsepower.

Though normally produced as a dozer, the D11R can be specially factory ordered as a tractor only, minus all of its bulldozing hardware. Pictured is one of these 850 flywheel horsepower D11R tractors pulling a modified 651E scraper unit with a custom-built dolly. *Urs Peyer*

In early 1996, the D11N was replaced by the improved D11R model series. Though initially the D11R was rated at 770 flywheel horsepower, the same as the N model, it would soon be increased to 850 in 1997.

Released in 1986, the D11N was the replacement model for the original D10 track-type tractor. It is shown here equipped with Caterpillar's optional giant hydraulic Impact Ripper. *Thomas Wilk*

The D11R is one of the most productive dozers ever released by Caterpillar. With its 850 flywheel horsepower diesel engine and massive 45-cubic-yard bulldozing blade, no job is too big for the D11R.

A D11R dozer equipped with a single-shank, deep-ripping arrangement has a maximum penetration depth of 7 feet 2 inches below the ground surface.

Caterpillar's D11R dozers can be found working in mining operations the world over. This particular D11R is shown working in Australia and is equipped with extra railings and operator platforms to meet the local regions' safety regulations. *Urs Peyer*

The D11R is not only a fantastic dozing device, it is also equally impressive as a ripping machine. The massive standard ripper on the D11R also acts as a counterweight to the unit's massive bulldozing blade.

In late 1996, Caterpillar introduced a second
D11R model called the Carrydozer. The D11R CD
Carrydozer was designed to meet customers'
demands for a bulldozer well suited to large
volume dozing applications. *Urs Peyer*

The 850 flywheel horsepower D11R CD Carrydozer features a specially designed bulldozing blade capable of carrying a portion of its load inside the curvature of the blade. This increased traction allows the Carrydozer to push a larger pile of material. *Urs Peyer*

Caterpillar Ultra-Large Track-Type Tractors				
Model	Build Year	Engine	Horsepower Gross/Flywheel	Weight (pounds)*
D10	1977	D348	—/700	191,100
D11N	1986	3508 DITA	817/770	205,948
D11R	1996	3508B EUI	935/850	230,935
D11R CD	1996	3508B EUI	935/850	248,600

*operating weight with blade and ripper

Early front-end loader attachments for Caterpillar diesel tractors were supplied by the Trackson Company of Milwaukee, Wisconsin. Pictured is a 1948 vintage D2 (5U) equipped with a cable-controlled Trackson T2 "Traxcavator" loader front-end.

The Trackson Company's first hydraulic loader design was the HT4 "Traxcavator" from 1950. It was designed to fit the Caterpillar D4. In December 1951, Caterpillar purchased the Trackson Company outright. Pictured is a Caterpillar HT4 (35C). This model would remain in production until mid-1955. Its replacement was the No. 955C (12A). *Author's collection*

The Trackson Company first started supplying Caterpillar with pipelaying tractor attachments in 1936. Vertical elevator–type loaders followed in 1937.

Caterpillar's largest front-engine track loader was the model 983 from 1969. In late 1978, a B series of the popular track loader was released. The 983B would eventually be replaced by the rear-engine, hydrostatic drive model 973 in early 1982. *Urs Peyer*

Caterpillar's largest current track-type loaders utilize a hydrostatic drive system, which eliminates the need of a gear-type transmission, steering clutches, and a final drive case. In their place are hydraulic fluid piston pumps and motors.

The 955 series of track loaders was a long-running, very successful model line for Caterpillar, dating back to 1955 with the 955C. The last version of this loader to be produced was the 955L (13X), which ended its run in 1981. *Author's collection*

Today, all of Caterpillar's larger track loaders are of a rear-engine, hydrostatic drive nature. The largest of these is the 973C, which was introduced in 2000. *Urs Peyer*

Caterpillar engineers originally tested various rubber-belted track configurations on a modified 130G motor grader rear chassis in 1980. It was referred to as the "Belt Track Test Bed", or "BTTB" for short.

The original Challenger 65 agricultural tractor was officially launched by Caterpillar in 1986. Featuring the innovative rubber Mobil-trac System (MTS), the Challenger offered far less ground compaction than comparable rubber-tired tractors of the day. *Caterpillar Inc. Corporate Archives*

In 1986, Caterpillar introduced a special agricultural track-type tractor called the AG6. It featured a variable horsepower Cat diesel engine and a special undercarriage, repositioned cab, and fuel tank for better balance.

For most of the 1990s, the Challenger 85 series was Caterpillar's most powerful MTS tractor. Originally introduced in 1992 as the 85C, it was upgraded in 1996 to the slightly more powerful 85D.

In 1997, Caterpillar took the wraps off an entire new lineup of redesigned E series MTS Challenger tractors. The most powerful of these was the 95E, which was rated at 410 gross horsepower.

The Hard Mobile Launcher (HML) was an experimental vehicle built by Caterpillar and Martin-Marietta in 1985 for the United States Air Force. The HML, which utilized Caterpillar's Mobil-trac System, was designed for land-based deployment of the nuclear ICBM Midgetman missile.

One of the more unusual tractor designs to feature MTS was the Deployable Universal Combat Earthmover, better known as the "DEUCE," which was built for the U.S. Army. After successful prototype testing of two units in 1996, limited contract production commenced in 1997.

Motor Graders

Motor Graders

As the need for better roads increased in the 1920s, equipment such as road graders became an important part of the equation in the building and maintenance of these projects. One of the industry leaders in road grader designs of the day was the Russell Grader Manufacturing Company of Minneapolis, Minnesota. Founded in 1903, Russell had been at the forefront of building various types of road maintenance equipment including blade graders, drag and wheel scrapers, and plows. In 1919, the company built the industry's first self-propelled grader, which would go into production as the Russell Motor Hi-Way Patrol No. 1 in 1920. This early powered grader utilized a modified Allis-Chalmers tractor. Later models would use tractors built by Fordson, Cletrac, and McCormick-Deering. In late 1926, Caterpillar entered the picture when it supplied its 2-Ton crawler tractor for use with the Russell Motor Patrol No. 4 grader. Another Caterpillar tractor, the Twenty, was

also utilized in the Russell Motor Patrol No. 6 in 1928.

The sales success of the Russell Motor Patrols featuring the Cat 2-Ton tractor did not go by unnoticed by Caterpillar. In a bold move, the company started negations with Russell in 1928 as to the possibility of purchasing the grader firm. By August of that year, a deal had been struck where Caterpillar would purchase Russell outright. After the purchase, Caterpillar discontinued all product lines that did not feature a Cat tractor model. Also, any parts of the old Russell business that were not related to the grader product lines were sold off. Equipment lines retained by Caterpillar included self-propelled, tractor-pulled, and elevating graders.

Now that Caterpillar had a complete line of pull-type graders to match to their tractors, the company's engineers went to work on a new type of self-propelled grader model. In 1931, the fruits of this labor were unveiled in the form of the Caterpillar Auto Patrol—the

On pages 76–77: As mining haulers get larger, so do the haul roads they travel on. To maintain these wider roads, only the largest motor grader will do: the Caterpillar 24H.

earthmoving industry's first true rubber-tired, self-propelled production motor grader. What made the Auto Patrol so significant was that the drivetrain and grader attachment were designed as a single unit, with the engine mounted in the rear for better balance and operator visibility. Even though the tractor-pulled and elevating graders continued to be marketed by the company until the early 1940s, the Auto Patrol concept was clearly the future for all new designs of the company's graders from 1931 onward.

By the end of 1931, Caterpillar's new motor grader became known as the No. 9 Auto Patrol. Other models were quick to follow. These included the No. 7 in 1932, the No. 10 in 1933, and the Diesel Auto Patrol in 1934. In mid-1936, the Diesel Auto Patrol became the Diesel No. 11, and a Diesel No. 10 was added to the product line. More modern designs included the No. 12 in 1938, and the No. 112 and No. 212 in 1939. Of all the early graders, the No. 12 stands out from the rest. In fact, the

12-series is the longest-running motor grader model line in continuous production today for the company.

Caterpillar's motor grader product lines have expanded over the decades and have been the standard to which all other makes and models are compared to. Key product line introductions over the years have included the 14B in 1959, the mighty 16 in 1963, the 120 in 1964, the 140 in 1970, and the 135H and 160H in 1995. Also introduced in 1995 were the all-wheel-drive 143H and 163H graders. Largest of all the company's motor grader offerings is the massive 24H. Officially introduced in 1996, the 24H is currently the world's largest production motor grader.

Caterpillar's H-series motor graders are some of the finest graders ever designed by the company's engineers. But soon they will be eclipsed by the even more productive new M-series machines featuring low-emission Cat ACERT diesel engines and state-of-the-art joystick operator controls.

The Caterpillar No. 11 Auto Patrol was first made available in late 1932. The original No. 11 was gasoline powered and used a single rear-drive axle. *Nick Cedar*

The Caterpillar Auto Patrol of 1931 was the earthmoving industry's first true self-propelled motor grader, built from the ground up with the blade attachment and drivetrain built as a single integral unit.

The original Caterpillar Auto Patrol was introduced in 1931. Starting in 1934, tandem rear-drive axles were offered as an option. *Author's collection*

In 1933, Caterpillar added the gas-powered No. 10 Auto Patrol to its growing lineup of self-propelled motor grader offerings. *Caterpillar Inc., Corporate Archives*

In mid-1936, Caterpillar introduced the Diesel No. 11 Auto Patrol. Though the model was offered with a single-drive axle, the majority of the units sold were equipped with tandem drive.

Caterpillar introduced the Diesel Auto Patrol in 1934. Though initially sold as a stand-alone model, it was reclassified as the Diesel No. 11 Auto Patrol in 1936. Both were equipped with a Cat D6100 diesel engine. *Caterpillar Inc., Corporate Archives*

In 1934, Caterpillar started offering the option of tandem-drive axles for all of its Auto Patrol models, which reduced the loping or bouncing ride nature associated with single-drive axle configurations.

The addition of tandem-drive axles, such as on this Diesel No. 11 Auto Patrol from 1937, improved the ride quality considerably. *Caterpillar Inc. Corporate Archives*

The 2 series is Caterpillar's longest-running motor grader model line, dating back to 1938. The 12H, introduced in 1995, proudly continues on this tradition of excellence today. *Caterpillar Inc.*

The No. 12 was Caterpillar's first motor grader model to feature leaning front steering wheels—to counteract side-draft caused by grading forces at the blade—as standard equipment. Previously, this feature was an option on older grader designs.

One of the more influential Caterpillar motor grader designs was the model No. 12. Released in mid-1938, the No. 12 featured a triple-box section frame and leaning front wheels as standard. It was available in tandem-drive configurations only. *Caterpillar Inc. Corporate Archives*

There have been numerous models of the No. 12 motor grader built over the decades. The No. 12F featured power-boosted steering and brakes and hydraulically leaned front wheels. It was introduced in 1965. *Author's collection*

The Caterpillar G-series of motor graders from 1973 were the company's first grader designs to feature an articulated frame for better maneuverability.

The original 14 series of motor graders was introduced in 1959 as the No. 14B. The modern 14H is large enough for the big road jobs, but is also ideally suited for construction jobsites as well. The 14H is rated at 220 flywheel horsepower.

Released in 1961 as the replacement for the No. 14C, the No. 14D motor grader featured positive mechanical controls and a 150 flywheel horsepower diesel engine. It was replaced by the No. 14E in 1965. *Caterpillar Inc. Corporate Archives*

The Caterpillar 140H introduced in 1995 replaced the 140G, which had been in service since 1973. The 140H features a 165-flywheel-horsepower diesel engine and a 12-foot-wide moldboard. *Caterpillar Inc.*

Caterpillar's 140H and 160H motor graders are also available in all-wheel-drive versions, the 143H and 163H. They were officially introduced in early 1995 at the same time as the 140H and 160H.

The 160H motor grader is slightly larger than the 140H series. The 160H features a 180-flywheel-horsepower diesel engine and a 14-foot moldboard, 2 feet wider than the standard 140H. *Caterpillar Inc.*

The 16H is the second-largest motor grader model in Caterpillar's product line, just behind the 24H. It is powered by a 265-flywheel-horsepower Cat diesel engine.

Introduced in 1963, the No. 16 was Caterpillar's first motor grader design to feature hydraulic power-actuated mechanical blade controls.

The big Caterpillar No. 16 motor grader was officially released in 1963. With its 225-flywheel-horsepower diesel engine, it was the most powerful Cat grader of its day. *Author's collection*

The 16H motor grader replaced the previous model, the 16G, in 1995. The 16H features a 16-foot-wide moldboard and a rear-mounted multi-shank ripper.

The largest Caterpillar motor grader at this time is the 24H. With its 24-foot-wide moldboard, it is capable of doing the work of two 16H units.

Caterpillar Large Motor Graders

Model	Build Year	Engine	Horsepower Gross/Flywheel	Blade (feet)	Weight (pounds)
No. 16	1963	D343	—/225	14/16	48,000
16G	1973	3406B	288/275	16	60,150
16H	1995	3196 ETA	299/285	16	69,648
24H	1996	3412E	540/500	24	136,611

The 24H is powered by a Cat 3412E diesel engine rated at 500 flywheel horsepower and is the most powerful grader model ever produced by the company.

The 24H is not only Caterpillar's largest motor grader, it is also the largest production grader built by anybody available to the world mining marketplace today.

Scrapers

Scrapers

As Caterpillar's track-type tractors started to be used more for heavy construction work and less as agricultural tools, many allied equipment manufacturers started designing and building various heavy-duty earthmoving attachments for these models. The kinds of equipment used on the company's tractors during the 1930s and 1940s included bulldozing blades, winches, rippers, and pull scrapers. During this time period, Caterpillar was not in the market of producing these kinds of attachments and depended on its allied suppliers, such as R. G. LeTourneau, for such equipment. During World War II, it was a common sight to see Caterpillar tractors equipped with LeTourneau bulldozer blades and Carryall pull scrapers being used by the Allies in all theaters of the war. But just before the war's end, Caterpillar decided that the time was right for it to start manufacturing its own designs of attachments, which would include scrapers.

In 1946, Caterpillar launched all new product lines of cable-controlled towed scraper designs. The first models of these included the No. 60, No. 70, and No. 80 series types. In 1949, the smaller hydraulically controlled No. 40 was added to the product line. The largest scraper of all, the No. 90, rounded out the company's offerings in 1951.

Caterpillar further strengthened its scraper lines by adding new designs of self-propelled wheel tractor scrapers. The company built its first rubber-tired tractor, the DW10, back in late 1940. But at the time, it was usually featured with a LaPlant-Choate or R. G. LeTourneau scraper unit, since Caterpillar did not build a scraper model yet. By 1947, the DW10 was finally equipped with a Caterpillar-designed No. 10 scraper. In late 1950, the company further strengthened its hand in the self-propelled scraper marketplace with the introductions of the DW20 and DW21. The DW20 utilized a two-axle tractor configuration like the smaller DW10. The DW21, on the other hand, used a single-axle tractor design.

Starting in 1959, Caterpillar introduced an entirely new model series of self-propelled scraper offerings referred to as the "600-series." The first of this new series was the model 619B. This was followed in 1960 by the larger 630A and 631A. But that was only the beginning. The year 1962 saw no fewer than seven model introductions, including the company's first twin-engine models. New single-axle tractor models included the 641, 651, and 657. Two-axle tractor models were the 632, 650, 660, and 666. Of these new models, only the 657 and 666 used a front- and rear-engine configuration. Other popular twin-engine model introductions included the 627 in 1968 and the 637 in 1970.

During the early 1960s, Caterpillar also started the introduction of a new type of scraper configuration. Referred to as an elevating scraper, the first model to feature this new design was the J619 in 1964. Other elevating types included the J621 in 1965, the 633 in 1966, the 613 in 1969, the 615 in 1982, the 623 in 1972, and the largest of them all, the 639D in 1979.

Today, Caterpillar is the undisputed global leader in the production of wheel tractor scrapers. The company faces competition from only a handful of manufacturers concerning its smaller scraper offerings. No other equipment builder today produces scrapers that threaten Cat's largest model offerings. Their really only competition is older Cat scraper units. Models such as the 637, 641, 651, and 657 series never seem to wear out. It is not an uncommon sight to find an early vintage 1960s model still hard at work at a jobsite today. There are even fleets of 666 and 666B units, Cat's largest scraper model ever, scattered across the western part of the United States, on standby waiting to be called back to work for large earthmoving contracts as needed.

Caterpillar's scraper legacy continues on today in the form of the G-series. The most modern and productive scrapers in the company's history, models include the 621G, 623G, and 627G, all introduced in 2000. Further releases include the 631G and 637G in 2001 and the company's largest, the 657G, in late 2005.

Caterpillar's first rubber-tired tractor designed for pulling a scraper or other earthmoving trailers was the DW10. Early models, such as this vintage 1947 DW10, were often attached to an R. G. LeTourneau LP Carryall scraper unit.

When Caterpillar originally introduced the DW10 rubber-tired tractor in 1940, it was usually equipped with a LeTourneau– or LaPlant-Choate–manufactured scraper unit. This was because Caterpillar did not build a scraper model of its own at that time.

The original DW10 was unveiled by Caterpillar in late 1940, with full production getting underway in 1941. The early designs of these tractors featured rounded metal fender fabrications. *Author's collection*

The next size up from the DW10 was the DW15 tractor series. Released in 1954, the DW15 was often paired up with the 12.5-heaped-cubic-yard No. 15 scraper unit. *Caterpillar Inc. Corporate Archives*

The first wheel tractor scraper model produced by Caterpillar to feature a single-axle tractor unit was the DW21. Officially introduced in late 1950, it was rated at 15-struck/19.5-heaped cubic yards. *Author's collection*

Caterpillar's DW20 and DW21 self-propelled scraper models were first publicly unveiled at the construction equipment Road Show, held in Chicago, Illinois, in August 1948.

The DW21 was originally paired with the No. 21 scraper unit. In 1955, the model was upgraded into the DW21C, with the scraper unit now becoming the No. 470. *Caterpillar Inc. Corporate Archives*

Introduced at the same time as the DW21, the DW20 featured a two-axle tractor design. It pulled the No. 20 scraper unit rated at 15-struck/20-heaped cubic yards capacity. *Peterson Tractor*

Since their introduction in 1959, the Caterpillar 600-series of self-propelled scrapers have dominated the earthmoving industry the world over. Shown is a current 631G at work. *Caterpillar Inc.*

The first 600-series tractor scraper model to be introduced was the 619B in 1959. The 619B was based largely on the experimental DW16 scraper program from 1958.

The original Caterpillar 631A wheel tractor scraper made its first appearance in 1960. Scraper operations were hydraulic and cable in nature. With the introduction of the 631B in 1962, all of the scraper functions became fully hydraulic. *Author's collection*

The 631B scraper's bigger brother was the model 641. Released in 1962, the 641 was rated at 28-struck/38-heaped cubic yards. The 641B was the last of the series, which ended production in 1981. *Author's collection*

The first two Caterpillar scraper models to be equipped with twin drivetrains were the 657 and 666, both in 1962.

The twin-engine–powered Caterpillar 627 series was originally released in 1968. The "B" version would make its official debut in 1974 and was rated at 14-struck/20-heaped cubic yards capacity.

The latest offering for the model 627 is the "G" series. Officially released in 2000, the 627G shares its front tractor design with the 621G and 623G scraper lines. *Caterpillar Inc.*

The larger twin-engine 637G looks very similar to the 627G. The original 637 series began production in 1970. The current "G" series model was introduced in 2001. Capacity is 24-struck/34-heaped cubic yards. *Urs Peyer*

The largest and most powerful custom-built Caterpillar scraper was the Peterson Triple 657. Built in 1965, it featured three 657 units hooked together and controlled by a single operator.

The largest and most powerful wheel tractor scraper manufactured by Caterpillar today is its massive 657G. Introduced in 2005, the tractor unit is equipped with a Cat C18 ACERT diesel engine (600 flywheel horsepower maximum), while the rear scraper gets the C15 ACERT diesel (451 flywheel horsepower maximum). *Caterpillar Inc.*

Dating back to 1962, the 657 series was Caterpillar's first single-axle tractor scraper model to utilize a twin engine concept and all-wheel-drive. The 657E series started its run in 1982.

The 657E scraper's rated capacity is 32-struck/44-heaped cubic yards. Its maximum combined power output from both engines is 1,045 (605/440) flywheel horsepower.

The 666 scrapers single-engine model counterpart in the product line was the 660. It would become a B series in 1969. The 660/660B tractor could also be ordered with dual-tire drive wheels. *Author's collection*

Caterpillar offered a special-order high-capacity coal-stockpiling scraper starting in 1967. The 70-cubic-yard 666 featured a single-axle 657 tractor front. This model was never advertised by the company for general sale.

With the same capacity as the model 666, and with only 500 flywheel horsepower to work with, the 660 usually needed the aid of pusher tractors to achieve decent loading times. *Caterpillar Inc. Corporate Archives*

First seen in 1962, the model 666 has the distinction of being the largest standard capacity scraper series ever offered by Caterpillar.

Caterpillar Large Wheel Tractor-Scrapers

Model	Build Year	Engine	Horsepower Gross/Flywheel	Capacity (yard^3) Struck/Heaped
657	1962	D346 (T)	—/500	32/44
		D343 (S)	—/400	
657B	1969	D346 (T)	—/550	32/44
		D343 (S)	—/400	
657E	1982	3412E (T)	632/605	32/44
		3408E (S)	457/440	
657G	2005	C18 ACERT (T)	632/600	32/44
		C15 ACERT (S)	478/451	
666	1962	D346 (T)	—/500	40/54
		D343 (S)	—/400	
666B	1969	D346 (T)	—/550	40/54
		D343 (S)	—/400	
Triple 657	1965 (Peterson)	D346 (x3)	—/1,500	—/150
		D343 (x3)	—/1,080	

The model 666 was rated at 40-struck/54-heaped cubic yards in capacity, with a 128,000-pound average load weight. In comparison, the 657 at the time was capable of carrying 104,000 pounds. *Urs Peyer*

The 666 scraper's front and rear engine's combined output was 900 (500/400) flywheel horsepower. In 1969, an improved 666B model was introduced with more power. It was rated at 950 (550/400) flywheel horsepower combined.

Wheel Loaders and Dozers

Wheel Loaders and Dozers

During the 1950s, Caterpillar continued to add new product lines to its growing roster of earthmoving equipment offerings. Caterpillar's "Traxcavator" track-type front-end loaders had become very popular in the marketplace. Management decided that the expansion of the front-end loader concept was in order to keep up with market demands for a faster and more versatile type of machine. But instead of tracks, it would have rubber tires.

In the mid-1950s, full developmental work started on the company's rubber-tired wheel loader program. By 1956, a prototype example identified as the model T101, was shown to management. Impressed with what they saw, the full go ahead was given to proceed to the next level of designing and building a full production line of wheel loader models. By 1959, the first production model was officially introduced by the company, the model 944A "Traxcavator." The 944A was a rigid frame design and steered with its rear wheels. Initially, diesel- and gasoline-powered versions of the 944A were produced. But

soon the gas version would be discontinued, leaving the diesel engine as the powertrain of choice. The 944A was an instant success with dealers and customers alike. Soon, both smaller and larger models would be added to broaden the wheel loader product line and enable Caterpillar to take on the industry's other wheel loader manufacturers head-to-head in the marketplace.

In 1960, Caterpillar introduced the models 922A and 966A loader lines. Both of these new designs featured a rigid frame and rear-wheel steering layout, just like the 944A. In 1963, major introductions in the loader product line included the new 988 and 966B models. Both of these loader designs now featured an articulated frame for steering. From now on, all midsize and large wheel loader designs would be of this steering configuration.

Caterpillar not only introduced the company's first articulated wheel loaders in 1963, but also introduced its first two models of articulated frame steering wheel dozers in that same year: the 824 and 834 model series. Not long after the introduction of the

834, a compactor model variation was released featuring optional sheepsfoot or tamping foot steel wheels. The revised model 824B was also available in a compactor configuration. But by 1970, both of these variations would be assigned new model nomenclature to better differentiate the dozers from the compactors. The 824B compactor became the 825B and the 834 compactor became the 835 series. Later on, special landfill compactors were introduced. The first of these were the models 826C in 1978 and 836 in 1993.

Caterpillar took a big leap up in size in 1968 with the introduction of its 992 wheel loader. The 992 was built for heavy high-volume loading operations typically found at large construction, quarry, and mining sites. The 992 was an immediate success. Over the years, the 992 series of wheel loaders has been the best-selling machine of its size the world over. The only loader built by Caterpillar larger than the 992 model series is the 994. Originally introduced in late 1990, the 994 is primarily marketed to larger mining operations.

Caterpillar's success in the highly competitive wheel loader marketplace led the company to investigate other rubber-tired loader designs, such as the backhoe tractor loader. The market for this type of loader had been dominated over the years by agricultural farm tractor manufacturers. But in 1985, Caterpillar introduced its first backhoe loader model in the form of the 416. This would be followed by the 426 and 428 model lines in 1986. Over the years, numerous models of backhoe loaders have been released by Caterpillar. Today, the company's E-series backhoe loaders are some of the most advanced machines of that type available to the construction industry.

Another variation to the rubber-tired loader theme is the skid-steer loader. Caterpillar introduced an entire new product line of compact skid-steer loaders in 1999, which, like the backhoe loader, is a very competitive marketplace. But the highly advanced designs of the company, along with its strong dealer and rental network, quickly established the Caterpillar skid-steer loader as a machine to be reckoned with.

Caterpillar's first production front-end, rubber-tired wheel loader was the model 944A "Traxcavator" of 1959. The 2-cubic-yard-capacity loader used a rigid frame and steered with its rear wheels. *Caterpillar Inc. Corporate Archives*

In 1960, Caterpillar followed up its first wheel loader design with the larger model 966A. Like the 944A, the 966A used a rigid frame design. In 1963, it was replaced by the articulated frame steering 966B. *Author's collection*

The "Traxcavator" product name was originally used by Caterpillar to identify its track loader line. But it was also used to identify the rubber-tired loader line for a few years after its introduction in 1959.

Today's Caterpillar "H" series midsized wheel loaders are some of the most advanced models the company has ever released. The 6-cubic yard class 980H introduced in 2005 features a 318-flywheel-horsepower, low-emission Cat C15 ATAAC ACERT diesel engine. *Caterpillar Inc.*

Caterpillar's popular 980 series of wheel loaders went into full production in 1966. It was replaced by the model 980B in 1970. *Urs Peyer*

The versatile Caterpillar 966 series is the longest-running wheel loader model line in the company's history. The 966G Series II was introduced in 2003 and was replaced by the 966H in 2005. *Urs Peyer*

In 2000, Caterpillar introduced an updated G series of its immensely popular 988 wheel loader. The 988G featured a radical mono boom design first seen on the 992G.
Thomas Wilk

In 1970, after several years of prototype testing, Caterpillar introduced a special 988 Carry Loader model featuring a front and rear lift bucket configuration. But problems with the loader caused it to be withdrawn from the marketplace by the end of that same year.

Officially released in early 1963, the model 988 was Caterpillar's first large wheel loader model to feature articulated frame steering. *Caterpillar Inc. Corporate Archives*

The 988G was replaced in 2004 with a new H series. The 988H looked like the previous model, but was now powered by a low-emission Cat C18 MEUI ACERT diesel engine, rated at 475 flywheel horsepower. *Thomas Wilk*

Caterpillar's model 992 positioned the company squarely in the big leagues of large wheel loader design. Introduced in 1968, the 992 soon became the best-selling large mining loader series in the world. *Author's collection*

In 1973, Caterpillar engineers built an experimental 992 Gas Turbine Loader featuring a very high power-to-weight ratio. The large amount of fuel required to run the turbine, however, caused the program to be cancelled.

Caterpillar replaced its 992 series with an updated B model in 1973. The 992B loader's most notable feature was its use of a pin-on ROPS cab structure, giving the cab its distinctive rear slope look. *Caterpillar Inc. Corporate Archives*

The Caterpillar 990, introduced in 1993, was based largely on model 992D. Major differences were less horsepower and a smaller capacity bucket than the 992D. In 2006, a new 990H model was introduced. *Urs Peyer*

Unveiled at the 1996 MINExpo, the 992G was Caterpillar's first wheel loader to feature a large, one-piece, cast-steel, box-section lift arm instead of the more traditional two-arm boom design.

Caterpillar Large Wheel Loaders

Model	Build Year	Engine	Horsepower Gross/Flywheel	Capacity (yard^3)	Weight (pounds)
990	1993	3412	660/610	11	161,994
990 II	1995	3412E	675/625	12	168,617
990H	2006	C27 ACERT	687/627	12	171,642
992	1968	D348	—/550	10	127,200
992B	1973	D348	—/550	10	147,850
992C	1977	3412	735/690	13.5	194,950
992D	1992	3412C	755/710	14	196,557
992G	1996	3508B DITA	880/800	16	210,424

One of Caterpillar's most popular large wheel loader models was its 13.5-cubic-yard rated 992C. Released in 1977, it sold in huge numbers worldwide.

The 992C would be replaced by the 992D series in 1992. The new D model looked much like the previous model, but now featured a walkway over the left rear tire and joystick operator controls. *Urs Peyer*

Caterpillar made a big increase in the size of its wheel loader designs with the introduction of the model 994 in late 1990. Equipped with a 23-cubic-yard bucket, it was the largest Cat loader of its day. *Caterpillar Inc.*

Before the introduction of the 994 in late 1990, Caterpillar had used the designation on a one-of-a-kind 20-cubic-yard diesel-electric–drive wheel loader in 1969. When the experimental electric-drive programs were cancelled by Cat management, the early 994 program was terminated.

The 994 quickly became the best-selling ultra-large wheel loader model in the world mining marketplace. It could do the work that was normally reserved for a hydraulic front shovel excavator.

In late 1998, the 994 became the 994D. Though power and capacity ratings were similar to the previous model, the D version featured new joystick operator controls and an increased operating weight for stability.

One of the big stars of the 2004 MINExpo was the new 994F. The new F model featured a host of design improvements over its predecessor, including increased power and payload, and a new operator's cab.

Caterpillar 994-Series Wheel Loader

Model	Build Year	Engine	Horsepower Gross/Flywheel	Capacity (yard^3)	Weight (pounds)
994	1990	3516	1,336/1,250	23	390,300
994D	1998	3516B EUI	1,375/1,250	23	421,600
994F	2004	3516B HD EUI	1,557/1,438	25	429,303

The 994F loader's improved Cat 3516B HD EUI 16-cylinder diesel engine, rated at 1,577 gross/1438 flywheel horsepower, dramatically increased the power output over the previous model. *Urs Peyer*

The new 994F is capable of loading a 240-ton capacity 793C hauler in seven passes when equipped with its standard 25-cubic-yard bucket. *Caterpillar Inc.*

The articulated steering Caterpillar 824 wheel dozer was originally introduced in 1963. *Caterpillar Inc. Corporate Archives*

Caterpillar's first articulated wheel dozer models, the 824 and 834, were both released in 1963, the same year as the company's first articulated wheel loader designs.

Caterpillar designed the 830M wheel-type tractor for the U.S. military. Introduced in 1962, it was built to pull three different types of government-purchased pull-scrapers supplied by various other manufacturers. *Caterpillar Inc.*

The largest wheel dozer offered by Caterpillar during the 1960s was its model 834. Designed and built at the same time as the smaller 824, the 834 also featured articulated frame steering. *Author's collection*

The 824 series of wheel dozers have been in continuous production since their release in 1963. The 824G Series II was originally introduced in 2002. It was replaced by the 824H in early 2005. *Urs Peyer*

Caterpillar Mid-Size Wheel Dozers

Model	Build Year	Engine	Horsepower Gross/Flywheel	Weight (pounds)
824	1963	5.4x6.5-cu-in 4-cylinder	280/250	62,400
824B	1965	D343	—/300	62,400
824C	1978	3406	340/315	58,435
824G	1995	3406C	340/315	58,697
824G II	2002	3406E	380/339	63,325
824H	2005	C15 ACERT	401/354	63,325
834	1963	D343	—/400	87,875
834B	1982	3408E	486/450	103,000
834G	2000	3456	525/481	103,849
834H	2005	C18 ACERT	554/498	103,849

Caterpillar has been building soil compactors almost as long as wheel dozer models. The latest 825H, which replaced the 825G Series II in 2005, uses a new low-emission Cat C15 ACERT diesel engine. *Caterpillar Inc.*

The 834G model series replaced the previous 834B wheel dozer in late 2000. The new model featured an improved drivetrain, cab design, and joystick operator controls. It would be replaced by the 834H in early 2005.

Tiger Engineering introduced its first wheel dozer model in 1982 as the model 690A. The 690A dozer's drivetrain was largely based on the successful Caterpillar 992C wheel loader.

Tiger Engineering Pty, Ltd., of Australia, in cooperation with Caterpillar, produced specially built wheel dozers based heavily on 992C/D wheel loader components. Released in 1993, the Tiger 690D featured a 20-foot 3-inch-wide blade.

Another Tiger-built wheel dozer was the 590B, which was based on components from the 990 Series II wheel loader program. After Caterpillar purchased the rights to this dozer from Tiger, it became the model 844. *Thomas Wilk*

Caterpillar's largest wheel dozer currently is the powerful model 854G. Officially introduced in 1998, the 854G is the largest wheel dozer ever offered by the company. *Caterpillar Inc.*

Caterpillar Large Wheel Dozers

Model	Build Year	Engine	Horsepower Gross/Flywheel	Weight (pounds)
590 (Tiger)	1994	3412	660/590	154,988
590B (Tiger)	1996	3412E HEUI	675/625	152,619
844	1998	3412E HEUI	675/625	152,619
690B (Tiger)	1985	3412	735/690	183,248
690D (Tiger)	1993	3412C	755/710	197,900
790D (Tiger)	1996	3508B	880/800	218,756
854G	1998	3508B EUI	880/800	219,128

The 854G originally started life as the Tiger 790G from 1996. After Caterpillar purchased the rights to the Tiger 790G in 1997, it was re-released in 1998 as the Caterpillar 854G.

The 854G wheel dozer is based around the drivetrain of the 992G wheel loader. Both the loader and dozer use a Cat 3508B EUI diesel engine rated at 800 flywheel horsepower and feature joystick operator controls.

In early 1999, Caterpillar introduced an entirely new product line of compact skid-steer loaders. In 2003, upgraded B model series were introduced across the line. Shown is a 268B equipped with the High Flow XPS load sensing, pressure compensating system.

Caterpillar's compact skid-steer loaders were introduced in 1999, along with a series of compact wheel loaders and mini-hydraulic excavators. These new smaller-sized machines were marketed toward smaller contractors and the very profitable equipment rental marketplace.

Caterpillar introduced a new line of compact multi-terrain loaders in 2001 featuring a rubber track undercarriage. In 2003 new B models were introduced. The rubber track undercarriage offers greater floatation, traction, and stability with far less ground pressure.

Caterpillar's largest backhoe loader offering is the 446 model series. Introduced in 1989, other model series include the 446B in 1993 and 446D in 2004. Power rating for the D model is 102 flywheel horsepower. *Caterpillar Inc.*

In early 2006, Caterpillar officially launched its new state-of-the-art E-series backhoe tractor loaders, featuring new cab and operator controls and a new backhoe design with an optional extendable stick.

Caterpillar entered the backhoe tractor loader market in 1985 and quickly established itself as a major player in a very competitive marketplace. The 420D IT (Integrated Toolcarrier) shown features a quick coupler that enables the loader to make a quick connection to selected work tools, such as specialized buckets, loader forks, brooms, rakes, and angle blades.

Off-Highway Haulers

Off-Highway Haulers

As the 1950s progressed, larger and larger fleets of off-highway haulers dotted the earthmoving landscape. Manufactured by respected heavy-equipment builders, they were a key factor in all projects of the day. The one problem with this was none of these trucks were a product of Caterpillar. It was a problem voiced by many of the company's top dealers. What the customers wanted was a one-stop source for their equipment needs. Since Caterpillar had no true off-highway truck to offer, the business automatically went to a competitor. Caterpillar management was well aware of the problem. The only solution was to start a new off-highway hauler program from scratch.

In the past, Caterpillar's popular DW21 single-axle tractor was used by many customers as a rear-dump hauler. When attached to a rear-dump trailer, or rocker, they became a very effective means of hauling material on a jobsite. But they were far from ideal, especially where top-haul road speeds and stability were concerned. For the industry at large, a rigid frame rear-dump truck was the only practical solution for maximum jobsite productivity.

By 1959, Caterpillar had its first prototype off-highway hauler. Though only a test mule at this stage, it would supply Caterpillar engineers with valuable engineering data. With this information in hand, further prototypes were built and tested. By November 1962, the company had a truck design it felt was production worthy. That truck was the 35-ton-capacity model 769. The 769 off-highway hauler would go into full production in 1963 and would be at the forefront of a series of new truck designs that would turn the earthmoving marketplace upside down.

After the introduction of the 769, Caterpillar set its sights on far larger truck designs featuring a diesel-electric drivetrain. These models of electric-drive haulers were the 75-ton 779, 100-ton 783, and 240-ton 786. All were designed at the same time and used many of the same drivetrain components, including the engine. All three models started testing in 1965. But the use of the Cat-designed diesel-electric drivetrain components proved troublesome for the trucks in the field. Caterpillar ended its early electric-drive program in late 1969, which also ended all three diesel-electric truck lines in the process. It was decided by management that full developmental resources should be concentrated at mechanical drivetrain truck designs for the foreseeable future.

Caterpillar got back on the right track with its truck program in 1970 with the introduction of the 50-ton-capacity 773. In 1971, a tractor version of the 773, the 772, was introduced for pulling bottom-dump trailers. But the company did not stop there. In 1974, the 85-ton capacity 777 made its debut in the marketplace featuring an all new front-end design. It would be the design look of all the company's hauler releases for the next 30 years.

Over the last 20 years, numerous quarry and mining off-highway truck designs have been launched by Caterpillar. In 1984, the company introduced the 785 series, and in 1986 the 789. Both of these designs were targeted at the mining industry. In 1991, the 793 was introduced and was the first 240-ton class hauler ever to be designed around a mechanical drivetrain. Caterpillar would again flex its engineering abilities in late 1998 with the unveiling of the 797. The nominal 360-ton capacity 797 was crowned the world's largest mechanical drive truck, a title it still holds today with the current 797B hauler, whose nominal payload capacity is 380 tons plus.

Even though the giant mining haulers received the lion's share of the limelight, new quarry-sized trucks were also introduced at a record pace. New product lines such as the 771 and 775 series were introduced as slightly larger capacity versions of the 769 and 773 model series, respectively. Heading into the twenty-first century, Caterpillar offers the most complete and technologically advanced line of off-highway haulers ever seen by the company. It is no wonder the company's trucks are number one in the off-highway hauler marketplace.

Caterpillar's first production off-highway rear-dump haul truck model was the 35-ton capacity 769 series. Introduced in late 1962, it would soon become the industry's dominant hauler in its size class. *Author's collection*

In late 1966, an upgraded B series of the 769 was introduced. The new 769B featured a redesign of the dump body to a V-bottom configuration, which helped eliminate rear-end spillage and allowed the use of larger tires. *Author's collection*

Opposite, top: The 769 series was one of Caterpillar's best-selling off-highway hauler lines from the 1960s through the 1990s. The 769D model replaced the previous 769C in late 1995. The 769D haulers capacity is a nominal 40-ton payload. *Urs Peyer*

Opposite, bottom: The 771D off-highway hauler is based largely on the 769D but has a greater payload capacity of 44.7 tons. This series of quarry trucks was originally introduced in 1992 as the 771C. *Urs Peyer*

Caterpillar's first true off-highway truck, the 769, was unveiled in November 1962. It went into full production in early 1963.

Caterpillar's 65-ton capacity class 775 series was originally launched in 1992 as the 775B. The 775 is based largely on the 60-ton 773 series. The 775E shown was released in 2001 and is now rated as a 70-ton class hauler. *Urs Peyer*

The model 773E is another one of Caterpillar's outstanding off-highway quarry trucks. The 773E originally replaced the previous 773D in 2001 and carries a nominal 60-ton payload capacity. *Caterpillar Inc.*

In mid-2006, Caterpillar introduced all new 773F, 775F, and 777F off-highway quarry trucks into the marketplace. The F-series haulers feature all new cab and front-end designs, and low-emission Cat ACERT Diesel engines.

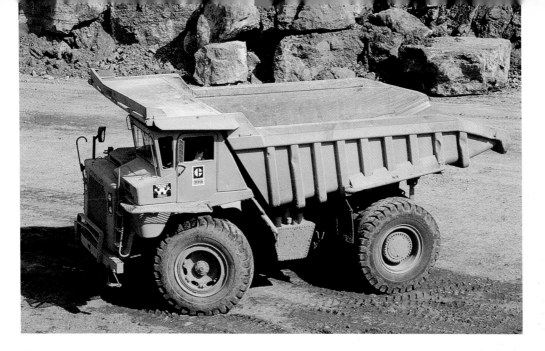

The original 773 off-highway rear-dump hauler was introduced in 1970. At the time of its introduction, it was rated at 50 tons in capacity. The model 773 was replaced by the 773B in 1978. *Urs Peyer*

For pulling various types of bottom-dump trailers, Caterpillar introduced a tractor version of the 773, identified as the 772. Released in 1971, it would be replaced by the 772B in 1979. *Author's collection*

Caterpillar's most popular off-highway tractor model is its 776 series. Originally introduced in 1976, the 776 is based on the chassis of the model 777 hauler and was designed to pull 150-ton capacity coal bottom-dump trailers. *Urs Peyer*

Caterpillar Large Off-Highway and Quarry Trucks				
Model	Build Year	Engine	Horsepower Gross/Flywheel	Capacity (tons)
773	1970	D346	—/600	50
773B	1978	3412	682/650	50
773D	1996	3412E	682/650	58
773E	2001	3412E	710/671	60
773F	2006	C27 ACERT	740/703	60
775B	1992	3412	682/650	65
775D	1995	3412E	725/693	69
775E	2001	3412E	760/730	70
775F	2006	C27 ACERT	787/740	70
777	1974	D348	—/870	85
777B	1985	3508	920/870	95
777C	1992	3508	920/870	95
777D	1996	3508B EUI	1,000/938	100
777F	2006	C32 ACERT	1,016/938	100

The 777 series is one of the most popular off-highway haulers in the 100-ton payload class. The model 777C pictured replaced the 777B in 1992. The original 777 was unveiled in 1974 as an 85-ton hauler. *Urs Peyer*

In 1996, the 777C was replaced by the 777D series. The 777D was powered by a Cat 3508B EUI diesel engine rated at 938 flywheel horsepower and carried a nominal payload capacity of 100 tons. *Urs Peyer*

In late 1966, after months of field testing, Caterpillar started limited production of its model 779 series diesel-electric drive off-highway hauler. In 1968, the payload capacity of the 779 was raised from 75 to 85 tons. Shown in this 1968 photo is a production 779 ready for delivery. *Author's collection*

Caterpillar's early electric-drive hauler program was headed up by Ralph H. Kress, who was hired in 1962 as manager of truck development for the company. Kress had formerly been employed by LeTourneau-Westinghouse and had been the designer of the first "Haulpak" truck in late 1956.

The original prototype 779 diesel-electric drive hauler program started testing in August 1965. Early dump body configurations for the 779 consisted of a rear-dump design and this side-dump model. *Author's collection*

The three-axle 783 was designed at the same time as the 779 series. Rated at 100-tons capacity, the electric-drive 783 steered with its front and rear wheels. The original side-dump 783 was built in 1965. In 1967, it had its body replaced with a rear-dump design. Only one 783 prototype was ever built. *Author's collection*

The largest of the early Caterpillar diesel-electric drive off-highway haulers was the massive 786 Coal Hauler. The prototype 240-ton capacity experimental 786 was built in late 1965. *Author's collection*

Caterpillar Early Electric-Drive Trucks				
Model	Build Year	Engine	Horsepower Gross/Flywheel	Capacity (tons)
779	1965	D348	1,000/960	75
779 (Production)	1967	D348	1,000/960	85
783	1965	D348	1,000/960	100
786	1965	D348 (x2)	2,000/1,920	240

The prototype 786 featured two powered tractors, which allowed the giant bottom-dump coal hauler to be driven from either end. Total power output of the two tractors was 1,920 flywheel horsepower. *Author's collection*

In 1968, the 786 entered limited production with four units being built featuring redesigned tractors with relocated engine modules. After the electric-drive program was canceled in late 1969, the 786 haulers were pulled from service. In all, only five units (including the prototype) were manufactured. *Author's collection*

The Caterpillar 785C is another one of the company's standout off-highway hauler designs. Powered by a Cat 3512B EUI diesel engine rated at 1,348 flywheel horsepower, it sits at the top of the 150-ton hauler class. *Caterpillar Inc.*

The original mechanical drivetrain–based 785 and 789 series of mining trucks were built to take on competing manufacturers haulers in the 150- to 200-ton capacity class, which had long been dominated by diesel-electric–drive designs.

The original 785 series was introduced in 1984 and was rated as a 130- to 150-ton capacity haul truck. In 1992, the 785 became the 785B and featured a power output of 1,290 flywheel horsepower. It would be replaced by the C model in 1998. *Urs Peyer*

The original 789 model series started production in 1986. In 1992, it would be upgraded into the 789B. The 789C pictured would enter service in 1998 and is rated as a 170- to 195-ton capacity hauler. *Urs Peyer*

The Caterpillar 793 series of haulers are the world's best-selling trucks in the 240-plus-ton-capacity class.

No one single recent Caterpillar off-highway hauler design has surprised the industry more than when the 793 series was introduced in 1991. The 793 featured a 240-ton capacity and a mechanical drivetrain. It would become the 793B in 1992.

The 793D was originally unveiled by Caterpillar at the 2004 MINExpo. Production started on the D model in late 2005. *Caterpillar Inc.*

The 793C XQ (Extra Quiet) mining truck features an innovative sound reduction package for mining regions with stringent environmental noise restrictions. The special radiator uses a hydraulically driven twin fan design. *Caterpillar Inc.*

In late 1998, Caterpillar took the wraps off the biggest Cat of all, the mighty 797. The 797 was the largest off-highway hauler ever offered by the company and is the world's largest mechanical-drive truck.

Caterpillar Mining Trucks

Model	Build Year	Engine	Horsepower Gross/Flywheel	Capacity (tons)
785	1984	3512	1,380/1,290	150
785B	1992	3512 EUI	1,380/1,290	150
785C	1998	3512B EUI	1,450/1,348	150
789	1986	3516	1,800/1,705	195
789B	1992	3516 EUI	1,800/1,705	195
789C	1998	3516B EUI	1,900/1,791	195
793	1991	3516	2,160/2,057	240
793B	1992	3516 EUI	2,160/2,057	240
793C	1996	3516B EUI	2,300/2,166	240+
793D	2004	3516B HD EUI	2,415/2,337	240+
797	1998	3524B EUI	3,400/3,211	360+
797B	2002	3524B EUI	3,550/3,370	380+

The 797 mining truck's payload capacity was listed at 360-plus tons, but it regularly carried loads approaching 400 tons. Power output of the 797 was 3,211 flywheel horsepower.

In 2002, the 797 was released in an upgraded B series. The 797B was rated at 380-plus tons capacity. But under the right conditions, it can easily handle loads in excess of 400 tons. *Urs Peyer*

The Caterpillar 3524B EUI 24-cylinder engine powering the 797B was developed by combining two 12-cylinder Cat 3512 powerplants in-line by means of an innovative flexible coupling system. This allows both engines to utilize a single crankshaft.

Big and powerful, the 797B has it all for an ultra-hauler. The truck itself is 32 feet wide to the outside of the rear tires and is just over 47 feet long. With a full load on board, it can attain a top speed of 42 miles per hour on level ground. *Urs Peyer*

Below: To power a mining truck as large as the 797B, you need a very big motor. The 117.1-liter displacement Cat 3524B EUI, 24-cylinder, 4-stroke diesel engine is rated at 3,550 gross/3,370 flywheel horsepower.

Caterpillar's articulated-hauler line originated with DJB Engineering's articulated trucks back in 1974. DJB haulers featured major drivetrain components supplied by Caterpillar and were sold and serviced through Cat's worldwide dealer network.

Caterpillar's articulated haul trucks can trace their origins back to DJB Engineering, Ltd. of England. In 1974, DJB introduced its first articulated hauler based on a Cat drivetrain. In 1985, Caterpillar acquired all the rights and designs to the DJB truck lines. The 30-ton-capacity D300E shown was originally introduced in 1995. *Urs Peyer*

Along with the three-axle models, DJB also designed a range of two-axle articulated haulers. Many of these designs would also become full Caterpillar models. Pictured is a 25-ton capacity D25C from 1985. *Author's collection*

The D400E Series II entered service in 1999 as an upgrade to the previous model D400E. Rated at 405 flywheel horsepower, it was capable of hauling a 40-ton payload. *Urs Peyer*

The highly capable Caterpillar 740 articulated haul truck was first introduced in 2001 as a replacement for the D400E Series II. As of 2006, the 740 model's rated payload capacity is 42 tons.

Caterpillar Modern Articulated Haulers

Model	Build Year	Engine	Horsepower Gross/Flywheel	Capacity (tons)
725	2000	C11 ACERT	309/301	26
730	2000	C11 ACERT	325/317	31
735	2001	C15 ACERT	408/385	36
740	2001	C15 ACERT	457/436	42

Caterpillar started introducing completely new designs of its popular articulated truck ranges in 2000. The first two models released were the 725 and 730. The 730 hauler's rated payload capacity is 31 tons. *Urs Peyer*

Along with the standard rear-dump design, the 740 is available with an ejector body. The 740 Ejector actually pushes its load out the back, on the move or standing still. The dump body does not rise on this model. *Urs Peyer*

Hydraulic Excavators

Hydraulic Excavators

The increased earthmoving and road-building contracts of the 1950s and 1960s ushered in numerous types of machinery concepts not seen before this time. One of these was the hydraulic excavator. Many companies that had for decades built contractor-sized cable-type backhoes and shovels were quickly finding ways of supplementing their older designs with new hydraulic type machines. It was during this time of change in North America that established manufacturers of hydraulic excavators in Europe and Asia saw great opportunity in the marketplace. Caterpillar management realized that if it did not act quickly, this new market would be lost to overseas competitors. So in the late 1960s, Caterpillar started the development of an entirely new line of hydraulic excavator designs to meet the new challenge head-on.

In early 1969, Caterpillar engineers unveiled a full-size wooden mock-up of a hydraulic excavator concept to management. Impressed with what they saw, the full go-ahead was given to proceed to a working prototype machine. By January 1970, an experimental 3/4-cubic-yard-capacity excavator, identified as the 625X1, was unveiled. Though further study and refinement was necessary, this prototype unit would eventually lead to Caterpillar's first production hydraulic excavator design, the model 225.

Caterpillar's model 225 excavator was officially launched into full production in 1972. It was quickly followed by the 235 series in 1973 and the much larger model 245 in 1974. To further broaden its new product line, a smaller model 215 series was introduced in 1976. Sales for all of these models were strong worldwide. To help meet customer demands in Europe, front shovel versions of the 235 and 245 were introduced in 1978 and 1976, respectively.

But as popular as the 225/235/245 excavators were, increased global competition and a crippling economic recession in the early 1980s forced Caterpillar into making new alliances with other manufacturers of hydraulic excavators. Starting in 1984,

On pages 170–171: Caterpillar is one of the leading manufacturers of hydraulic excavators in the earthmoving industry today. The 375 L ME (Long-undercarriage Mass Excavator) was designed for large scale jobs requiring a 7-cubic-yard machine. *Urs Peyer*

Caterpillar started marketing a series of smaller excavators produced by Eder of Germany. The early models included the 205 LC, 211, and 213. Model types that used a wheeled undercarriage included the 206, 212, 214, and 224. But of greater importance was the company's longtime alliance with Mitsubishi Heavy Industries. Caterpillar's relationship with Mitsubishi dated back to 1962 when the two companies formed an equal-ownership and manufacturing and marketing company for the production of certain types of Cat track-type tractors and wheel loaders. In 1987, this partnership was expanded to include hydraulic excavators. The first excavator models to be built by Shin Caterpillar Mitsubishi Ltd. included the E70, E110, E120, E140, E180, E240, E300, E450, and E650. This close working relationship between Caterpillar Inc. and Shin Caterpillar Mitsubishi Ltd. would eventually lead to a whole new generation of excavator designs known as the 300-series.

In early 1992, the new 300-series of excavator models started to make their way into the marketplace. The earliest releases included the models 320, 325, and 330. In 1993, the larger 350 and 375 series were introduced. These models proved to be some of the finest hydraulic excavators ever offered by Caterpillar. Over the years, numerous other models have been added to the product line. The largest of these is the 385B series, which replaced the previous model 375 in early 2002. Recent releases of 300-series excavators include the 324D, 325D, and 330D, all in early 2006.

For larger quarry and mining customers, Caterpillar offered the 5000-series of large hydraulic excavators. Available in front shovel and backhoe configurations, they were some of the best-selling machines in their respective size classes. The first of the series to be released was the 5130 front shovel in 1992. In 1993, a backhoe version was also introduced. The largest of the 5000-series was the model 5230. It was released in 1994 in front shovel form and in 1995 in a backhoe version. Other 5000-series excavators included the 5110B in 2000, the 5080 (based on the model 375) in 1994, and its replacement, the 5090B (based on the 385B series) in 2002.

But even though Caterpillar's big mining excavators sold well in the marketplace, their project start-up costs were enormous. And future research and development was also going to cost millions of dollars. These were funds that management felt could be put to better uses elsewhere in the company. So in 2003, Caterpillar discontinued the 5110B, 5130B, and 5230B excavator product lines. Of all the 5000-series models, only the 5090B remained as the front-shovel version of the 385B backhoe excavator.

Caterpillar originally entered the hydraulic excavator marketplace in 1972 with the model 225. Largest of the early hydraulic designs was the model 245, which was released in 1974. *Author's collection*

Between 1972 and 1984, Caterpillar essentially sold only four model types of hydraulic excavators—the 215, 225, 235, and 245 series.

The original Caterpillar 235 hydraulic excavator was introduced in 1973. In 1978, a front shovel version was released with a 2.38-cubic-yard bottom-dump bucket. *Caterpillar Inc. Corporate Archives*

The 245 series was also released in 1976 in a front shovel configuration. Equipped with a bottom-dump bucket, it was rated at 4 cubic yards. While sold in North America, the early Cat front shovels primarily targeted the European marketplace. *Caterpillar Inc. Corporate Archives*

Along with crawler-type excavators, Caterpillar offers a limited number of wheeled designs. The M318C MH (Material Handler) shown is equipped with a hydraulic cab riser. *Urs Peyer*

In 1987, Caterpillar offered two large Mitsubishi-sourced hydraulic excavator models, the E450 and E650. Both excavators were available in backhoe and front shovel configurations and were primarily built for the Asian marketplace.

Caterpillar hydraulic excavators come in all shapes and sizes. The 321C LCR features a compact radius design, enabling it to work in urban construction jobsites where space is often restricted. *Urs Peyer*

The Caterpillar 345B L FS Series II front shovel was primarily built for the European marketplace. Launched in 2003, it carries a 3.2-cubic-yard bottom-dump bucket. *Thomas Wilk*

For the North American marketplace, Caterpillar offers over 68 different types of hydraulic excavators as of 2006. From small to large, front shovels to material handlers, Cat builds hydraulic excavators to fit every job description imaginable.

The 345B L excavator was originally released by Caterpillar in 1997, and it has proven to be a favorite in the marketplace. Power output of the 345B L was listed at 321 flywheel horsepower. *Thomas Wilk*

In early 2005, Caterpillar officially released an improved model 345C L excavator featuring a new low-emission, 345-flywheel-horsepower Cat C13 ACERT diesel engine. The unit shown is equipped with an optional quick-change bucket attachment system. *Urs Peyer*

Like other 300-series hydraulic front shovels, the 365B L FS Series II is primarily built for the European marketplace. Officially released in 2003, the model is rated at 404 flywheel horsepower and is equipped with a 5.2-cubic-yard bucket. *Urs Peyer*

Front shovel versions of Caterpillar's 345- and 365-series of hydraulic excavators are primarily intended for the European marketplace and are not marketed in North America.

The first 365B L series of excavators was originally introduced by Caterpillar in 1999. That model would in turn give way to the 365B L Series II in 2002. In early 2005, the 365C L ME was released with a Cat ACERT diesel engine. *Caterpillar Inc.*

In 2005, an improved 365C L FS hydraulic front shovel model was introduced by Caterpillar in Europe. The new model now featured a low-emission Cat C15 ATAAC ACERT diesel engine rated at 404 flywheel horsepower. *Urs Peyer*

Caterpillar officially released the 385B L excavator in early 2002, after months of successful field trial testing, as a replacement for the 375 L. Average bucket size of the 385B L was rated at 6 cubic yards. *Thomas Wilk*

Caterpillar Large Construction Excavators

Model	Build Year	Engine	Horsepower Gross/Flywheel	Capacity (yard³)	Weight (pounds)
345B L	1997	3176C	312/290	2.38	97,100
345B L II	2000	3176C	345/321	2.38	97,940
345B L FS II	2003	3176C	345/321	3.27	122,598
345C L	2005	C13 ACERT	—/345	2.46	99,150
350 L	1992	3306	—/286	3	111,377
365B L	1999	3196	—/385	3.6	149,000
365B L II	2002	3196	—/404	3.6	149,000
365B L FS II	2003	3196	—/404	5.2	161,715
365C L	2005	C15 ACERT	—/404	3.68	145,430
375 L	1993	3406C	455/428	5	181,500
385B L	2002	3456	—/513	6	190,370
385C L	2005	C18 ACERT	—/513	6	187,360

Available at the same time as the standard 385B L model was a larger capacity mass excavator configuration. The shorter boom-equipped 385B L ME was capable of handling a 7.75-cubic-yard bucket. *Urs Peyer*

Various optional tools and special booms are available for most of Caterpillar's larger hydraulic excavators. Pictured is a 385C L (released in early 2005) equipped with a demolition sheer attachment. *Urs Peyer*

The Caterpillar 5090B is actually the front shovel version of the 385B excavator series. Released in 2002, the 5090B is specially suited for the European marketplace, where front shovels of this size are very popular. *Thomas Wilk*

The 5090B is slightly larger than the previous 5080 it replaces and carries a larger 7.4-cubic-yard bucket. It is also more powerful with 513 flywheel horsepower now available. *Thomas Wilk*

For customers looking for large mining-type excavators, Caterpillar allows many of its dealerships worldwide to market the Terex-O&K line of RH-machines, which are some of the largest hydraulic excavators in the world.

Caterpillar's original model 5080 Front Shovel started life in 1994. Based on the 375 excavator series, it had a power output of 428 flywheel horsepower and was equipped with a 6.8-cubic-yard bucket. *Urs Peyer*

Caterpillar officially launched a production version of the 5110 as the 5110B in 2000. With a standard bucket capacity of 9.9 cubic yards, it was well suited for loading trucks in the 50- to 60-ton-capacity class. The 5110B ended production in late 2003. *Thomas Wilk*

Only seven backhoe excavators—and one front shovel version—of the original 5110 series were ever built, and all were considered preproduction machines leading up to the release of the 5110B.

In 1996, Caterpillar started the field testing program on a new hydraulic excavator line, the model 5110. The pilot 5110 backhoe's capacity range was 8.4 to 9.5 cubic yards for the mass excavator configuration. *Caterpillar Inc.*

Caterpillar released a single prototype 5110 FS front shovel in 1997 for field trial testing. Rated at 600 flywheel horsepower, the front shovel was equipped with a 9.8-cubic-yard bucket. *Urs Peyer*

Caterpillar's 5130B front shovel first entered service in late 1997. Bucket capacity for the B model went up from 13.75 cubic yards to 14.5. Power also increased from 755 flywheel horsepower to 800.

Caterpillar discontinued the 5110B, 5130B, and 5230B hydraulic excavator lines in late 2003. The only 5000-series machine left in the product line as of 2006 is the 5090B.

The first of Caterpillar's new line of large mining hydraulic excavators was the model 5130. Introduced in 1992, the first version to be built and released was the 5130 FS front shovel. *Urs Peyer*

In late 1993, Caterpillar introduced a backhoe version of the 5130. Rated at 10.2 cubic yards, the 5130 ME found immediate acceptance in the mining marketplace. *Urs Peyer*

The largest of Caterpillar's big hydraulic mining excavators was its 5230 series. Originally introduced in 1994, the 5230 FS front shovel's bucket carried a rated payload capacity of 22.2 cubic yards.

Caterpillar 5000-Series Excavators					
Model	Build Year	Engine	Horsepower Gross/Flywheel	Capacity (yard^3)	Weight (pounds)
5080	1994	3406C	455/428	6.8	184,800
5090B	2002	3456	—/513	7.4	192,900
5110 ME	1996	3412E	640/600	9.5	276,728
5110 FS	1997	3412E	640/600	9.8	271,215
5110B ME	2000	3412E HEUI	758/696	9.9	280,900
5130 ME	1993	3508	815/755	13	390,000
5130 FS	1992	3508	815/755	13.75	385,000
5130B ME	1997	3508B	860/800	13.7	401,000
5130B FS	1997	3508B	860/800	14.5	399,000
5230 ME	1995	3516	1,575/1,470	21	697,980
5230 FS	1994	3516	1,575/1,470	22.2	702,000
5230B ME	2001	3516B EUI	1,652/1,550	21	723,400
5230B FS	2001	3516B EUI	1,652/1,550	22.2	721,000

The backhoe version of Caterpillar's largest mining excavator was the 5230 ME. Introduced in 1995, the backhoe had the same 1,470-flywheel-horsepower rating as the front shovel version.

In late 2001, Caterpillar introduced a more powerful, 1,550-flywheel-horsepower upgraded version of its big front shovel model, the 5230B. Even though power was up, bucket capacity remained unchanged. In late 2003, the 5230B excavator program was discontinued.

INDEX